PENGUIN BOOKS
BEYOND THE SYLLABUS

Ankur Warikoo is an entrepreneur, teacher, content creator and bestselling author based in India. He creates content that resonates with young people aged 13 to 30, building a global community of over 15 million followers.

Since 2009, Warikoo has been building and leading startups. He currently runs WebVeda.com, an online school focused on life skills and personal growth. He is the author of four bestselling books: *Do Epic Shit*, *Get Epic Shit Done*, *Make Epic Money* and *Build an Epic Career*.

READ MORE BY ANKUR WARIKOO

Do Epic Shit
Get Epic Shit Done
Make Epic Money
Build an Epic Career

BEYOND THE SYLLABUS

The real-life guide for teenagers
who want more than just marks!

ANKUR WARIKOO

PENGUIN BOOKS

An imprint of Penguin Random House

PENGUIN BOOKS

Penguin Books is an imprint of the Penguin Random House group of companies whose
addresses can be found at global.penguinrandomhouse.com

Published by Penguin Random House India Pvt. Ltd
4th Floor, Capital Tower 1, MG Road,
Gurugram 122 002, Haryana, India

First published in Penguin Books by Penguin Random House India 2025

Text copyright © Ankur Warikoo 2025

All rights reserved

10 9 8 7 6 5 4 3 2

The views and opinions expressed in this book are the author's own and the facts are as reported by him
which have been verified to the extent possible, and the publishers are not in any way liable for the same.
Nothing in this book is intended to cause offence or to hurt the sentiments of any individual,
community, section of people, group or religion.

Please note that no part of this book may be used or reproduced in any manner for the
purpose of training artificial intelligence technologies or systems.

ISBN 9780143471103

Book design and layout by Supriya Bhandari
Typeset in Good Dog New
Printed at Replika Press Pvt. Ltd, India

This book is sold subject to the condition that it shall not, by way of trade or otherwise, be lent,
resold, hired out, or otherwise circulated without the publisher's prior consent in any form of
binding or cover other than that in which it is published and without a similar condition
including this condition being imposed on the subsequent purchaser.

www.penguin.co.in

Dedicated to all the years I spent feeling inadequate, incomplete and incapable. If only I had been patient with myself— as I would hope you will be, with yourself.

School teaches you about mitochondria and the Pythagorean theorem, which is 90% useless.

But no one tells you how to handle failure, make money before you turn 18, or stop overthinking that one text you sent at 2 a.m.

No one tells you how to make friends, how to handle break-ups, and that it's okay to lose your friends along the way.

No one tells you how to make decisions, how to process failure or how to build a successful life.

This book?
It's the stuff school will never teach you.

Some pages you'll vibe with, some will make you
roll your eyes, and some might just call you out.

No long chapters—nothing here is longer than
2 pages. No need to read in order. Just open
any page and . . . boom! Instant life hack.

It's short. It's fun.
It's the 'gyaan' you actually need.

Life doesn't come with a manual.
But this? Pretty close.

FIGURING OUT LIFE

The biggest myth about growing up?

THAT THERE IS ONLY ONE RIGHT WAY TO LIVE LIFE.

There isn't.

Some figure the way at 18.
Others at 40. Some chase big dreams,
others find happiness in simple things.

THERE'S NO FIXED PATH.
NO PERFECT TIMELINE.

YOUR VERSION OF

SUCCESS

doesn't have to look like anyone else's.

YOUR VERSION OF

SUCCESS

SHOULD BE YOURS ALONE.

The things that seem like a big deal
in school and college?
They barely matter a few years later.

Your rank, your popularity, that
one embarrassing moment in class—
ALL OF IT FADES.

WHAT LASTS?

The kind of person you become.

BEING AN ADULT MEANS NO ONE TELLS YOU WHAT TO DO.

That's the BEST PART and the HARDEST.

NO ONE HAS IT ALL FIGURED OUT.

There's no guaranteed formula for success.

Only trial, error, learning and unlearning.

You'll outgrow some dreams,
AND THAT'S OKAY.
What you wanted at 10 may
not be what you want at 20.

LET YOURSELF
→ CHANGE. ←
LET YOURSELF
GROW.

When you grow up, TIME is the only thing you'll wish you had more of.

SPEND IT ON WHAT ACTUALLY MATTERS.

PEOPLE WON'T ALWAYS UNDERSTAND YOUR CHOICES.

MAKE THEM ANYWAY.

As long as it feels right to you,
THAT'S ENOUGH.

No one tells you how much of life

TAKES
PRACTICE.

Not just studying or sports—
even making friends, dealing with
failure and setting boundaries.

EVERYTHING GOOD IN LIFE TAKES TIME.

You're not
LOST.
You're just early,
STILL
EXPLORING.

In school, asking too many questions
can sometimes get you dismissed.
In life, asking too many
questions is the
ONLY WAY TO GET AHEAD.

The smartest people
in the world never stop asking

QUESTIONS.

SCHOOL SAYS,

'DON'T COPY.'

LIFE SAYS,

'LEARN FROM THE BEST.'

You don't have to start from scratch.
Study what works for you, make it yours
and build from there.

A 'WRONG' DECISION ISN'T ALWAYS WRONG.

Sometimes, it's just the decision that TEACHES YOU THE MOST.

YOUR ABILITY TO LEARN

is more important than

WHAT YOU'VE LEARNED.

Most of what you've learned in school won't be useful in 10 years' time.

IN REALITY, SUCCESS IS BUILT IN THE HOURS NO ONE POSTS ABOUT.

In school, you're taught to

WAIT FOR PERMISSION.

In life, you often need to

TAKE ACTION WITHOUT IT.

No one is going to tell you

WHEN TO BEGIN.

If you wait for the
perfect moment,

YOU'LL WAIT
FOREVER.

THE FEAR OF LOOKING STUPID STOPS MORE PEOPLE THAN FAILURE EVER WILL.

It's okay to be bad at something new. That's how you get good.

The people who keep GROWING IN LIFE?

They're not the ones who
always make the

BEST DECISIONS.

They're the ones who aren't

AFRAID TO CHANGE
THEIR DECISIONS

when the decisions stop making sense.

IF YOU DON'T CHOOSE FOR YOURSELF, SOMEONE ELSE WILL.

And their choices may not be in your favour.

Do not take

PERMANENT DECISIONS

based on

TEMPORARY EMOTIONS.

SUCCESS ISN'T A WALK DOWN A STRAIGHT ROAD.

It's a MESSY DANCE—sometimes forwards, sometimes backwards, sometimes in circles.

No one gives you a

MAP FOR LIFE.

YOU CREATE IT AS YOU GO.

Wrong turns, detours, dead ends—

THEY'RE ALL A PART OF THE JOURNEY.

MONEY AND INDEPENDENCE

The true purpose of

MONEY ISN'T TO BUY THINGS.

It is to give you the

FREEDOM TO CHOOSE.

Extra fries today. A solo trip tomorrow.
That gaming mouse now.
The freedom to take a gap year later.
A gift for your crush today.
The power to walk away
from a bad job tomorrow.

[MONEY ISN'T THE GOAL. FREEDOM IS.]

'Bro, I'm too young to think about money!'

'How much will I even make if
I start earning?'

'Studies first, money later.'

'No point starting small.'

BUT HERE'S THE THING...

INDEPENDENCE

isn't about

(HOW MUCH YOU HAVE.)

It's about knowing

YOU CAN MAKE IT ON YOUR OWN.

ASK YOURSELF:

- What do people always bug you to help them with?

- What's something that you're great at that others totally suck at?

- What takes you 10 minutes but takes them forever?

Whatever came to mind just now?
That's not just a

HOBBY.

That's a

SKILL.

And a skill =
money waiting to be made

Love designing?
Sell posters, logos, Insta templates.

Good at explaining?
Tutor or sell study guides.

Always joking?
Write captions for new and upcoming brands.

Obsessed with cricket?
Share fantasy league tips.

Techie? Teach elders WhatsApp, UPI
and Blinkit.

Love viral trends? Edit or script videos.

Got stuff lying around? Rent or sell it.

DON'T WAIT FOR A JOB. GET CREATIVE. GET EARNING.

THE WORLD PAYS YOU FOR THE VALUE YOU CREATE, NOT THE HOURS YOU WORK.

EARNING MONEY GIVES YOU CONFIDENCE.

It's proof that you can

RELY ON YOURSELF.

If you can't manage ₹500,
you won't be able to manage ₹1,00,000.

MORE MONEY DOESN'T FIX BAD HABITS. IT JUST MAKES THEM BIGGER.

You don't need
A DEGREE TO EARN.
You don't
EVEN NEED A JOB.

YOU JUST NEED A SKILL THAT SOMEONE ELSE FINDS VALUABLE.

DECIDE WHERE YOUR MONEY GOES, OR YOU'LL ALWAYS WONDER WHERE IT WENT.

A new phone?
₹20,000. Gone forever.
Investing that same ₹20,000?
Could be worth ₹2 lakh in 20 years.

The first choice keeps you stuck in
the cycle of earning and spending.
The second buys you freedom.

CHOOSE WISELY.

START EARLY—LET TIME DO THE WORK.

Start Age	Monthly Investment	Total Invested by Age 50	Your Bank Balance by Age 50
15	₹1,000 (increasing 10% annually)	₹22.8 lakh	₹1.18 crore
30	₹1,000 (increasing 10% annually)	₹12 lakh	₹16 lakh

Same investment. Same effort.
But 7X the money.

That's the power of compounding.
The earlier you start, the less you
need to invest to make more.

The best time to start?

YESTERDAY.

The second-best time?

RIGHT NOW.

Your neighbour says, 'Money is everything.'

Your parents say, 'Money is the root of all evil.'

Your teacher says, 'Money isn't important, focus on your studies.'

So, what's the truth?

MONEY ISN'T GOOD OR BAD—IT'S JUST A TOOL.

A tool that gives you options, choices and the ability to build the life you want.

Money won't
magically solve all your problems.

BUT NOT HAVING IT

CREATES A
WHOLE NEW SET
OF PROBLEMS.

SPENDING SMART > SPENDING LESS

SPENDING ISN'T BAD. THOUGHTLESS SPENDING IS.

- Buy what you love, not what FOMO tells you to.
- Get what you need, not just what's on sale.
- Spend on experiences, not just things you'll forget next week.

ALWAYS HAVE AN EMERGENCY STASH.

Life happens. Phones break.
Last-minute trips pop up.
Friends forget their wallets.

An emergency fund means

YOU DON'T HAVE TO PANIC OR BORROW.

Start small—₹500, ₹1,000
or whatever you can.

Because the only thing worse
than an emergency . . .
IS BEING BROKE WHEN IT HAPPENS.

That sale?
That limited-time offer?
That but-it's-50%-off
moment?

STILL DOESN'T MAKE IT A SMART BUY.

BECAUSE BEING BROKE WITH COOL STUFF... IS STILL BEING BROKE.

MONEY ISN'T JUST ABOUT GETTING, IT'S ALSO ABOUT GIVING.

Treat your parents to ice cream.
Buy a gift for a friend, just because.
Donate ₹100 to a cause you believe in.

IT'S NOT ABOUT THE AMOUNT,
IT'S ABOUT THE HABIT.

BECAUSE THE
HAPPIEST PEOPLE?

THEY DON'T JUST MAKE MONEY. THEY USE IT TO SPREAD GOOD.

YOUR FIRST EARNING > YOUR FIRST DEGREE

Not because of the amount,
but because of what it means.

Your first earning gives you

THE CONTROL

to say yes to what excites you.

THE POWER

to say no to what drains you.

THE MOMENT YOU REALIZE

YOU CAN STAND ON YOUR OWN.

The world defines wealth by

WHAT YOU OWN.

REAL WEALTH IS WHEN

NOTHING OWNS YOU.

The person with

₹10 LAKH IN THE BANK AND A SIMPLE CAR

IS RICHER THAN THE ONE WITH

₹1 LAKH AND A LUXURY–CAR LOAN.

THE BIGGEST FINANCIAL RISK? NEVER TAKING ONE.

Earning, investing and learning about money can feel scary at first.

[**BUT AVOIDING IT?**]

THAT'S HOW YOU STAY POOR.

RELATIONSHIPS AND SOCIAL LIFE

THE MOST IMPORTANT
RELATIONSHIP IN YOUR LIFE?

THE ONE YOU HAVE WITH YOURSELF.

EVERY FRIENDSHIP, EVERY RELATIONSHIP, EVERY CONNECTION...

It all starts with how you see yourself.

If you don't like yourself, you'll look for approval in the wrong places.

If you don't respect yourself, you'll settle for less than you deserve.

YOU BECOME LIKE THE PEOPLE YOU SPEND THE MOST TIME WITH.

CHOOSE WISELY.

Not everyone will like you,
AND THAT'S OKAY.

You don't need to change
who you are to fit in.

THE RIGHT PEOPLE WILL FIND YOU.

THE TRUE TEST OF FRIENDSHIP
isn't just who stays with you
during hard times.

IT'S WHO IS TRULY HAPPY FOR YOU WHEN YOU SUCCEED.

WANT TO BE INTERESTING? BE INTERESTED.

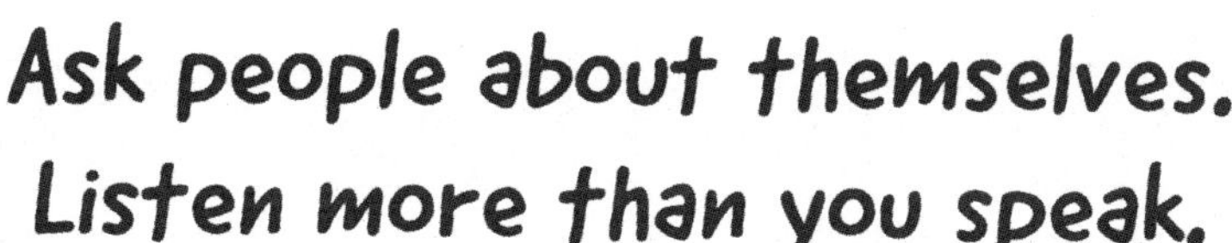

Ask people about themselves.
Listen more than you speak.

SOME FRIENDSHIPS
FEEL LIKE HOME.
OTHERS FEEL
LIKE A HABIT.

LEARN THE DIFFERENCE.

Real friends don't guilt trip you.

They don't make you
prove your worth.

THEY MAKE YOU FEEL SAFE EVEN WHEN LIFE ISN'T.

Some friendships don't
end with a fight.

[THEY JUST FADE.]

Being ignored hurts more than
hearing the truth.
But someone who ghosts you was
never really there.

IF THEY STOP SHOWING UP, BELIEVE THEM.

THAT'S YOUR ANSWER.

You will outgrow people.
It will feel strange at first—
like something is wrong.

BUT IT'S NOT.
IT'S GROWTH.

And not everyone grows
at the same pace.

LETTING GO DOESN'T MEAN YOU DON'T CARE.

IT MEANS YOU FINALLY CARE ABOUT YOURSELF.

BEING DIFFERENT IS A SUPERPOWER.

The things that make you feel out of place now?

They'll be your strengths later.

THE WORLD DOES NOT NEED ONE MORE TEMPLATE.

PEOPLE DON'T THINK ABOUT YOU AS MUCH AS YOU THINK.

You stress over what others will say. You overanalyse a text, a post or a conversation.

BUT HERE'S THE TRUTH:

EVERYONE ELSE IS TOO BUSY THINKING ABOUT THEMSELVES.

Stop living for their approval.
You're the only one who
has to live your life.

SETTING BOUNDARIES DOESN'T MEAN PUSHING PEOPLE AWAY.

It means knowing where to draw the line.

If someone makes you feel guilty for saying 'no', it's because they benefited every time you said 'yes'.

YOUR TIME AND
ENERGY AREN'T
UNLIMITED.
GIVE THEM TO
PEOPLE WHO
RESPECT THEM.

Some arguments are just a
WASTE OF TIME.
Not every fight needs your energy.

SILENCE IS OFTEN THE LOUDEST ANSWER.

BEING ALONE ISN'T THE SAME AS BEING LONELY.

The toughest person to sit with?

YOURSELF.

But once you enjoy your own company, you'll never feel lonely again.

PEOPLE LOVE HEARING THEIR OWN NAME.

Use it when you greet them.
Use it in a conversation.

THEY'LL FEEL
SEEN, HEARD AND REMEMBERED.

Attraction is easy.
LOVE TAKES EFFORT.

IF THEY ONLY CARE WHEN THEY NEED SOMETHING, THAT'S NOT LOVE— IT'S CONVENIENCE.

Love isn't measured in posts, captions or #couple goals.

IT'S HOW THEY TREAT YOU OFFLINE.

Families are complicated.

THEY WON'T ALWAYS GET YOU, BUT THEY WILL ALWAYS STAND BY YOU.

Flowers, chocolates, Valentine's Day—
cute, but not love.

LOVE IS IN THE LITTLE THINGS.

The random 'text me when you get home'.

The way they remember your favourite snack.

The good-luck message before your exam.

LOVE ISN'T ABOUT SHOWING OFF. IT'S ABOUT SHOWING UP.

DON'T BE IN A RUSH TO BE WITH SOMEONE.

Instead, crave to be with yourself.
If you feel incomplete alone, a
relationship won't fix it.
It will only distract you from it.

A RELATIONSHIP SHOULD ADD TO YOUR HAPPINESS, NOT BE YOUR ONLY SOURCE OF IT.

YOUR PARENTS
DON'T ALWAYS
HAVE THE
RIGHT WORDS.
BUT THEY HAVE THE
RIGHT INTENTIONS.

They grew up in a different world.
One where things weren't as
simple, fast or open.

They may not understand
everything you do,
but they want the best for you in
the only way they know how.

PARENTS MAY NOT ALWAYS SAY 'I LOVE YOU' OUT LOUD.

But they'll show it in a hundred different ways.

Saving you the last piece of food.

Scolding you for staying out late
but waiting up till you're home.

Checking if you've eaten,
even when they're upset with you.

Making you a snack when you study late.

Silently watching over you, always.

LOVE AT HOME IS HARDLY EVER SPOKEN. IT'S FELT.

THE ONE QUESTION THAT CAN STRENGTHEN ANY RELATIONSHIP: HOW CAN I DO BETTER?

A better friend. A better partner. A better teammate.

IT SHOWS YOU CARE.

It means you're listening, not just assuming.

And it's the simplest way to make any relationship stronger.

MINDSET AND MENTAL STRENGTH

Everything you do often becomes a habit.

If you keep doubting yourself,

YOU'LL ALWAYS HESITATE.

If you keep believing in yourself,

YOUR CONFIDENCE WILL GROW.

CONFIDENCE IS BUILT, NOT BORN.

The first time is always
the hardest.
The second time is easier.
The third time? You'll wonder
why you were ever scared.

FEAR DOESN'T VANISH. YOU JUST LEARN TO MOVE BEFORE IT STOPS YOU.

EVERY TIME
YOU STEP OUTSIDE YOUR
COMFORT ZONE,

YOUR
COMFORT ZONE
EXPANDS.

REJECTION ISN'T FAILURE. IT'S FEEDBACK.

Every 'NO'
teaches you something—
if you're willing to listen.

The people who succeed?

They hear ' no' more
than anyone else.

THEY JUST DON'T STOP AT A 'NO'.

Sometimes, rejection looks like
failing a test, not making a team,
or your friend ignoring you.
But it's not the end of the world.

THEY DIDN'T REJECT YOU.

They rejected an application.
A text message. A request.
A moment in time.

IT'S NOT THE END. IT'S JUST A REDIRECTION.

KEEP GOING.
THE RIGHT ' YES' IS
STILL AHEAD.

The happiest-looking people?
They cry, too.
They doubt themselves, too.
You just don't know about it.

EVERYONE IS FIGHTING BATTLES YOU DON'T SEE.

THE WORLD IS ALWAYS SELLING SOMETHING.

[A new look, a new trend, a new way to be 'better'.]

The second you stop comparing,
YOU START WINNING.

YOU'RE NOT HERE TO FIT IN. YOU'RE HERE TO BE THE BEST VERSION OF YOURSELF.

Not everyone will see your potential.
That doesn't mean it's not there.

PROVE THEM WRONG BY PROVING YOURSELF RIGHT.

YOU DON'T FIND YOURSELF. YOU BUILD YOURSELF.

→

BY TRYING, FAILING, LEARNING AND EVOLVING.

PROGRESS FUELS MOTIVATION.

A person doesn't feel happy just by achieving a goal.

A person is happy when they know they are moving towards a goal.

YOUR BRAIN NEEDS TO FEEL PROGRESS.

That's why video games are addictive.
That's why finishing a chapter
in a book feels good.

IF YOU DON'T TRACK YOUR PROGRESS, YOU'LL FEEL STUCK EVEN WHEN YOU'RE NOT.

MOTIVATION DOESN'T CREATE ACTION. ACTION CREATES MOTIVATION.

Waiting to feel inspired?
You'll be waiting forever.
START FIRST, and the motivation
will catch up.

Sad? Angry? Frustrated? Feel it.
Cry. Journal. Scream into a pillow.
Then let the feeling pass through you.

PAIN NEEDS AN EXIT, NOT A PERMANENT HOME.

YOU WON'T ALWAYS FEEL LIKE SHOWING UP. THAT'S OKAY. START SMALL.

Even tiny steps count.

Reading 1 page a day =
30 books in 5 years

Doing 10 pushups a day =
18,000 pushups in 5 years

Saving ₹10 daily = ₹18,000 in 5 years

TINY ACTIONS =
MASSIVE RESULTS
OVER TIME

WHEN THINGS GET HARD, DON'T QUIT. SWITCH IT UP.

Move to a new study spot or
just rearrange your old one.
Try a different workout.
Tackle the problem from a new angle.
Step outside. Get some sunlight.

SOMETIMES, YOU DON'T NEED MOTIVATION. YOU JUST NEED A CHANGE.

Stop saying, 'I should be further ahead.'
Ahead of what? Who made the rules?
There is no deadline for figuring out life.

YOUR TIMELINE IS YOURS.

Don't bottle it up. Talk to someone—
a friend, a sibling, a teacher or
a school counsellor who just gets it.

THE BRAVEST THING YOU CAN DO IS ASK FOR HELP.

The voice in your head?
Make sure it's your biggest cheerleader,
not your worst critic.

BECAUSE THE WAY YOU SPEAK TO YOURSELF MATTERS.

You wouldn't tell your best friend:
'You're so stupid.'
'You'll never be good enough.'
'You always mess up.'

THEN WHY DO YOU SAY IT TO YOURSELF?

TALK TO YOURSELF WITH THE SAME KINDNESS YOU SHOW OTHERS.

OVERTHINKING IS A TRAP.

Your brain creates a million scenarios.
99% of them never happen.

ASK YOURSELF:
- Will this even matter in 3 months?
- What's the worst that can happen?
- If this was happening to my best friend, what would I tell them?

YOUR MIND IS YOUR HOME. KEEP IT SAFE.

Don't let it be filled with self-doubt, negativity and fear.
Decorate it with self-respect, kindness and belief in yourself.

YOU ARE ENOUGH.

Not just when you get better marks.
Not just when you get into that college.
Not just when you have more friends.
Not just when you look a certain way.
Not just when you achieve more.

RIGHT NOW. AS YOU ARE.
YOU ARE ENOUGH.

THAT DOESN'T MEAN YOU STOP GROWING.

It means you already have everything you need to grow into whoever you want to be.

WORK AND FUTURE READINESS

No one in the real world cares about
your report card or marksheet.

THEY CARE ABOUT WHAT YOU CAN ACTUALLY DO.

YOUR ABILITY TO THINK, COMMUNICATE AND SOLVE PROBLEMS

will take you further than your grades ever will.

Your resume is just
a piece of paper.

YOUR SKILLS ARE THE REAL PROOF.

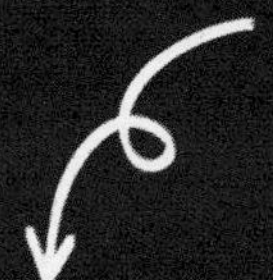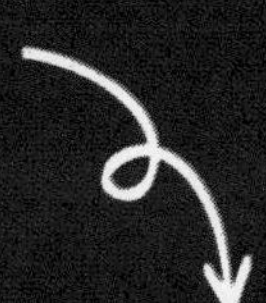

Stop waiting to
'BE DISCOVERED'.
PUT YOUR WORK
OUT THERE AND
PROVE WHAT
YOU CAN DO.

The best way to prove yourself?

SOLVE REAL PROBLEMS. FOR REAL PEOPLE.

Your attendance is not your success.

YOUR ATTENTION IS.

Your marks are not
your success.

YOUR UNDERSTANDING IS.

Your college admission is
not your success.

YOUR PROGRESS IS.

NO ONE OWES YOU A DREAM JOB.

But you can make yourself
valuable enough to earn it.

BE THE ONE WHO FINDS SOLUTIONS, NOT THE ONE WHO WAITS FOR INSTRUCTIONS.

You're NOT competing against

STUDENTS IN FANCY COLLEGES.

$\longrightarrow$

You're competing against those

WHO KNOW HOW TO GET THINGS DONE.

The real question isn't

'SHOULD I GO TO COLLEGE?'

It should be

'HOW DO I MAKE COLLEGE WORTH IT?'

Four years of just studying?

WASTED.

Four years of learning,
experimenting and
building something?

PRICELESS.

Use college to meet people. To try new things. To learn beyond the syllabus.

COLLEGE ISN'T JUST ABOUT ATTENDING, IT'S ABOUT GROWING.

Before choosing to go to college,
ASK YOURSELF:

DO I NEED IT FOR MY CAREER?

OR AM I JUST GOING BECAUSE EVERYONE ELSE IS?

A DEGREE CAN OPEN DOORS.

BUT ONLY YOUR SKILLS WILL HELP YOU WALK THROUGH THEM.

If college isn't your path,
don't just sit and wait.

LEARN. WORK. EXPERIMENT.

PROVE YOU DIDN'T NEED IT.

FAILURE IS NOT THE STEPPING STONE TO SUCCESS.

If that were true, everyone who failed would be successful.

THE MISSING PIECE?

REFLECTION.

FAILURE
+
REFLECTION
=
SUCCESS

If you think you will
end up a failure,

ISN'T IT BETTER TO FAIL DOING WHAT YOU TRULY WANTED TO DO?

The greatest skill in the 21st century?

THE ABILITY TO LEARN ANYTHING WHENEVER REQUIRED.

Want to deal better with failure?

PRACTICE FAILING.

Every day, pick a task with
A HIGH CHANCE OF FAILURE,
BUT A LOW COST OF FAILING.

Apply for a competition you think
you won't win.

Message someone you admire
(even if they don't reply).

Pitch an idea to someone who might say no.

Try to learn a skill that seems impossible.

Speak up in class, even if you're unsure.

WITHIN 30 DAYS, YOU WILL

START DEALING WITH FAILURE A LOT BETTER.

THE #1 PREDICTOR OF SUCCESS?

Not your college.
Not your grades.

IT'S CURIOSITY.

Your degree has an
expiry date.

YOUR CURIOSITY DOESN'T.

CURIOSITY CREATES MORE OPPORTUNITIES THAN HARD WORK EVER WILL.

The Internet lets you reach anyone.

The question is:

ARE YOU USING IT TO CONSUME OR TO CREATE?

Google is free. YouTube is free.

If you're not using them to

LEARN,

you're choosing to

STAY BEHIND.

AI CAN DO THE BORING WORK.

Use it to write better,
research faster and automate tasks.

FREE UP TIME FOR REAL LEARNING.

THE SMARTEST PEOPLE AREN'T SCARED OF AI.

They train it, use it
and get ahead because of it.

AI WON'T TAKE YOUR JOB.

BUT SOMEONE WHO KNOWS HOW TO USE AI WILL.

WHAT AI CAN'T REPLACE?

CREATIVITY. EMOTIONAL INTELLIGENCE. CRITICAL THINKING.

The BEST CAREERS will be built by people who

COMBINE THESE WITH AI SKILLS.

Your biggest advantage as a teen?

NO ONE EXPECTS YOU TO BE AN EXPERT YET.

That means you have time to get better—without the pressure.

Your POTENTIAL is just the starting point.

WHAT TRULY MATTERS IS WHAT YOU DO WITH IT.

DIGITAL LIFE AND THE REAL WORLD

'You have one new notification.'
'Someone liked your post.'
'Click the link to find out.'
AND SUDDENLY, HOURS DISAPPEAR.

'Post this.'
'Look like that.'
'Go viral or be invisible.'
AND SUDDENLY, YOU'RE CHASING
LIKES INSTEAD OF BEING YOURSELF.

ARE YOU IN CONTROL? OR IS SOCIAL MEDIA CONTROLLING YOU?

Most distractions feel harmless...

UNTIL YOU REALIZE THEY STOLE YOUR DREAMS.

SOCIAL MEDIA ISN'T FREE.

You don't pay with money.
You pay with time, attention
and self-worth.

NOT EVERYTHING ONLINE IS REAL.

Filters, edits, perfect lives—
it's a highlight reel. Not real life.

DON'T BELIEVE EVERYTHING YOU SEE.

SOCIAL MEDIA IS LIKE FOOD.

Some of it is good for you.
Some of it is junk.

WHAT YOU CONSUME DAILY SHAPES YOUR MIND.

When you scroll through
social media mindlessly, you are not
entertaining yourself.

You are not even numbing yourself.

[
**YOU ARE
LOSING
YOURSELF.**
]

How do you stop comparing your 'boring' life to their 'perfect' one? You feel disappointed because you crave what they have.

SO, CHANGE WHAT YOU CRAVE.

FOLLOW IDEAS, NOT PEOPLE.
FOLLOW INSPIRATION,
NOT ILLUSIONS.

YOU CONTROL WHAT YOU CONSUME.

GIVE YOUR BRAIN TIME TO BE BORED.

That's when your best ideas happen.

The best creators don't just post.

THEY LOG OFF AND LIVE A LIFE WORTH POSTING ABOUT.

THE MORE TIME
YOU SPEND
ONLINE, THE
LESS TIME YOU
SPEND LIVING.

LOG OUT. LOOK UP.

LIFE IS HAPPENING OUTSIDE THE SCREEN.

BE KIND ON SOCIAL MEDIA.

A truly happy person
will never troll someone.

DON'T WASTE TIME FIGHTING TROLLS.

They want attention.
Don't give it to them.

YOUR PHONE ISN'T THE PROBLEM; YOUR HABITS ARE.

Control your notifications
or else they will control you.

Every app fights for your time.

THE MORE YOU SCROLL,
THE MORE THEY WIN.

THE LESS YOU FOCUS, THE MORE YOU LOSE.

SOCIAL MEDIA ALGORITHMS [SIMPLY AMPLIFY OUR BELIEFS.]

THEY MAKE US A
BIGGER VERSION OF
OURSELVES.

NOT A BETTER VERSION OF OURSELVES.

THE INTERNET NEVER FORGETS...

EVEN IF YOU DO.

Before you post, ask yourself:

WOULD FUTURE ME BE PROUD OF THIS?

THE INTERNET GIVES EVERYONE A VOICE.

Some use it to lift others up.
Some use it to tear others down.

CHOOSE WISELY WHICH ONE YOU LISTEN TO.

IF YOU WOULDN'T SAY IT IN REAL LIFE, DON'T POST IT ONLINE.

A POST TAKES SECONDS.

A
SCREENSHOT
LASTS
FOREVER.

THE SECRET NO ONE TELLS YOU!

The dream life you want
won't just happen,
but you can make it happen.

YOU HAVE THE POWER TO CREATE IT.

Every choice, every action,
every thought—they're shaping your
future, whether you realize it or not.

What you say yes to,
what you walk away from,
what you spend time on,
what you let go of...

IT ALL
ADDS UP.

NO ONE IS LIVING THIS LIFE FOR YOU.

Every decision is yours to make.
Every win is yours to celebrate.
Every setback is yours
to learn from.

It might feel scary.
But it also means
you're in control.

YOU HAVE THE POWER TO CHANGE THINGS. AND THAT CHANGES EVERYTHING.

THE SOONER

you realize your decisions
affect you the most,

THE EASIER

it gets to make
the right ones.

Not the ones that impress others,
not the ones that feel safe,

BUT THE ONES THAT ACTUALLY TAKE YOU FORWARD.

MOST PEOPLE GO THROUGH LIFE BLAMING OTHERS.

'My parents forced me into this.'
'I had no choice.'
'Things just never worked out.'

BUT HERE'S THE TRUTH:
YOU ALWAYS HAVE CHOICES.
Even when things go wrong. Even when the
odds are against you.
Even choosing to do nothing is a decision.

YOU CAN TAKE CHARGE OR LET LIFE HAPPEN TO YOU.

LIFE ISN'T WAITING FOR YOU TO FEEL READY.

It's moving—right now, at this very moment. You're either in the driver's seat or being dragged along for the ride.

TAKE THE WHEEL. YOU'VE GOT THIS!

EVERYTHING YOU WANT IS ON THE OTHER SIDE OF SOMETHING HARD.

A dream job is on
the other side of 100 rejections.

A strong body is on
the other side of 100 workouts.

A great skill is on
the other side of 100 bad attempts.

A life you can be proud of is on
the other side of hard choices.

IF YOU AVOID DISCOMFORT, YOU'LL AVOID GROWTH.

YOU CAN'T CHASE EVERYTHING.

$\longrightarrow$

BUT YOU CAN CHASE WHAT ACTUALLY MATTERS TO YOU.

The sooner you figure that out,
the clearer your path becomes.

Took the wrong turn?
Google Maps doesn't yell at you.
It doesn't panic.

IT JUST REROUTES AND FINDS A NEW WAY FORWARD.

Life works the same way.

MISTAKES HAPPEN.
PLANS CHANGE.

AS LONG AS YOU
KEEP MOVING, YOU'LL GET WHERE
YOU NEED TO BE.

One day, you'll look back and realize
this moment was a choice.

THE CHOICE TO STAY THE SAME OR START SOMETHING GREAT.

And in that moment,
you won't be thinking about the fears, the
doubts or what people will say.

You'll only wonder:
'WHAT IF I HAD STARTED SOONER?'

But here's what matters:

YOU'RE HERE NOW.

This moment is yours.
This choice is yours.

AND YOU STILL HAVE THE POWER.

YOU JUST HAVE TO USE IT.

If you lived your whole life the way you lived it in the last 2 weeks, would it get better or worse?

THAT ONE QUESTION CAN CHANGE EVERYTHING.

YOU'RE NOT JUST A PLAYER IN THIS LIFE; YOU'RE THE CREATOR.

SO CREATE SOMETHING AMAZING.

LETTERS I WISH I HAD WRITTEN TO MY TEENAGE SELF

Dear ankur,

You turn 13 today.

Masi gifts you a book called the
' Big Book of Space'.
You are going to fall in love with it.
You will dream of becoming an astronaut and
working for NASA.

You will tell everyone about this dream.
Your school friends and teachers will know you
as the kid who wants to go to NASA.
It will become your identity.

But it is not your identity.
You are so much more than just a degree
or a job.
And I wish you knew that before you let this
dream define you completely.

You are going to be okay, ankur.
You are going to be okay :))

Dear ankur,

You turn 14 today.

Your voice is cracking.
There is a visible moustache now, but not
enough to call you a man.
You don't quite like your body any more.
Sometimes, you feel ashamed of it.
You hate it when your friends call you ' chikna'
because you don't have much body hair.
The boys at school talk about girls, and you have
nothing to say, nothing to contribute.

'Is something wrong with me?' you wonder.

You ask yourself this question more
than ever before.
But there is nothing wrong with you.
You are changing, and change isn't always easy.
But change is necessary.

I wish I could tell you that in 30 years, you will
be fitter than you have ever been, happier than
you have ever been, richer than you have ever
been and more popular than you have ever been.

But you don't know that today.
And that's okay. That is life.

You are going to be okay, ankur.
You are going to be okay :))

Dear ankur,

You turn 15 today.

This year, you will say goodbye to some really
close friends.
It's because you've chosen to study science,
and they haven't.
It makes you terribly sad. I get it.
You have spent years with them, and now you
might not even get a few hours together.
Your teachers will change.
Your schedule will change.
Everything will change.

And you are scared.
There are times you wish you were
not growing up.

But you will have to grow up.
And trust me, you are going to have a lot of fun
growing up.
You just don't know it yet.

You are going to be okay, ankur.
You are going to be okay :))

Dear ankur,

You turn 16 today.

You are deep into your IIT JEE preparation.
But Ma and Papa are not doing well financially.
So, you cannot afford that expensive
classroom coaching.

You didn't score enough to get into DPS either.
'I might not do well because I don't have what
others have,' you tell yourself.

You know what?
That's just an excuse.
Because you have things that a lot of
people do not have.
A family that loves you, cares for you and
provides you with food, shelter, education and
a safe environment.

Right now, you may not think that matters.
But one day, you'll realize it's the only thing
that really matters.

You are going to be okay, ankur.
You are going to be okay :))

Dear ankur,

You turn 17 today.

School is getting intense.
But you are also getting popular.
That shy kid from before is quickly turning into
a confident kid who participates in debates and
competitions and is known as an all-rounder.

But it also makes you judge others.
You judge those who smoke, drink and party.
You judge those who choose to study humanities
and commerce.
You judge those who bunk classes.

You feel superior because you believe
your way is the only right way.

But your way is just that—yours.
It does not have to be everyone's way.

Do not judge.
Because it is not what people do,
but who they are within, that defines them.

You are going to be okay, ankur.
You are going to be okay :))

Dear ankur,

You turn 18 today.

You didn't make it to IIT.
It broke you. Shattered you.
You cried.
Ma and Papa cried.
Everyone had pinned their hopes on you.
And you felt like you let them all down.

You join Delhi University while preparing
for the entrance exam again.
You still believe you can crack it.

But you know what, ankur?
That exam doesn't define you.
Those marks do not define you.
That college doesn't define you.
It feels like everything depends on this right
now, but one day you will realize that
it never did.

You are going to be okay, ankur.
You are going to be okay :))

Dear ankur,

You turn 19 today.

You did not make it to the IITs . . . again.
Two attempts gone.
You give in, focus on college and try to
get into the IITs for your master's degree.
But you know what?
You won't make it then either.

You will never crack any competitive exam.
But in 25 years, you will have visited every
big IIT in the country. They will invite you
as a speaker.

To address their students.
And show them how to live life.
Funny, isn't it?
How life comes full circle.
And that's the beauty of life.

You decide what defines you,
and that decides how the world sees you.

You are going to be okay, ankur.
You are going to be okay :))

Scan QR code to access the
Penguin Random House India website